One Minds' Book of
Incomplete Thoughts

Poetry and Other Thoughts

RUBY KOEVORT

This edition is published by
That Guy's House in 2018

© Copyright 2018, Ruby Koevort
All rights reserved.

No part of this publication may be reproduced, stored in a retrieval system, or transmitted, in any form or by any means without permission of the publisher.

www.ThatGuysHouse.com

Hey,

Welcome to this wonderful book brought to you by That Guy's House Publishing.

At That Guy's House we believe in real and raw wellness books that inspire the reader from a place of authenticity and honesty.

This book has been carefully crafted by both the author and publisher with the intention that it will bring you a glimmer of hope, a rush of inspiration and sensation of inner peace.

It is our hope that you thoroughly enjoy this book and pass it onto friends who may also be in need of a glimpse into their own magnificence.

Have a wonderful day.

Love,

Sean Patrick

That Guy.

*I asked "That Guy" to be my publisher!

Acknowledgements

For everyone that has entered my life, I thank you. It is the ordinary interactions and observations of everyday life that has offered me endless inspiration. Without these to ignite the spark, I would have had nothing to warm my soul and light the page.

Dianne Put, thank you for your keen eye, insight, and candor. You helped make this process a little less scary!

Lise Schulze, your authenticity and openness with play has given me the courage to step into my own. You are so appreciated by myself and our tribe. Thank you. You always love and see the best in people, and that is a gift beyond measure.

To the lovely Janice Butler, who I fondly refer to as my instigator. You have a way of gently pushing me past my own limitations. Anyone who has you in their corner has the best cheering squad!! You are a true gatherer of hearts! Thank you for not allowing me to hide.

Above all, my Bailey and Lane, you two are truly my greatest teachers. Thank you for always challenging me to be better than yesterday, to dream a bigger tomorrow, and enjoy today.

Ask The Questions

In this life I have truly come to grasp that inspiration and the divine messages can come from anywhere. Each day I am blessed with the gift of openly receiving without judgement (for the most part) for the delivery or of myself. Many messages are simply nudges that have me see things in a way I hadn't thought of before, and then there are others that stop me in my tracks and fill my heart and soul to an extent that it overwhelms and overtakes everything in that moment and often for many more to come. I was blessed with such insight the other day. What started as a heartfelt conversation with my son turned into a beautifully expanded melody a few days later. And with you I am very guided to share.

"How can the Universe have been created, when the Universe is Creation itself?"

"How can the Universe have been created, when the Universe is Creation itself?"

~ Lane Koevort (February 6, 2015 Age 8)

This most poignant question was the result of a most heartfelt conversation with my Lovely Son. How do you answer a question like that?

You don't.

Some questions are asked simply to raise the consciousness of humanity. Such inquiries manifest to set forth ripples. Ripples that will gently awaken the divinity in a few souls, this will ultimately awaken the consciousness of the masses. In the past there have been those precious few who dared to question aloud, knowing the answers would not be given in this time or on this plane of existence. These are stars sent forth to light the way to a more holistic way of being. Most will not, at this moment, find such questions as a sign post; however, there will be some that will run with it. This will in exchange bring forth the next level of existence on this plane. When faced with such messages, questions, this is the light coming forth to allow you to understand the paradox of your time.

Set forth. Ask the questions. Every such contemplation will bring arise to a higher vibration that will not be ignored by all.

Change is inevitable, because how can the Earth have been created....How can You have been created, when ALL is creation itself.

The Answer

Play with me Angel and show me the magic.
Let me play with your hair.
Let me hear your voice.
Allow me to hear the story and in it the answers.
Dance with me beyond the clouds,
and show me the stars that light your way.
Of these I have asked and of these I was answered....
I have
I do
I Will.

Thoughts...

In my own personal journey, I have found more than a few things to be almost absolutes for me. Though I wouldn't say there aren't more, or that one is more than the other. I only see them as a few of the main constructs of my observations that I seem to be bound to.

Love/heart, fear/courage, choice, acceptance/observation and Spirit are in no particular order for me. They do however work together, as all things, to help me create this life, this journey, that fills me. They guide me to the experiences that, though I may not want some of them, I need. Like a sapling searching for the warmth of the sun and refreshment of the spring rain, I search for the deeper wells of meaning and light to feed and nourish my soul.

I wouldn't say that Spirituality defines my life so much as it has shown me the greatness of my life and of all life. It is showered with observations, contemplations and gratitude. It has guided me to see what I perceive as flaws, as constricting and deluded. The brilliance of our gifts, which are obvious, inherently undervalued and repressed. It is less about the teachings and a destination and more about encompassing the journey and finding the lessons sprinkled within every blade of grass. As I sit back and watch so many suffering right now, I am pressed to remind us all that all our healing techniques, crystals and so forth, are only tools. Nothing more. All the love, forgiveness, healing, and so forth must start **within** our own being, for that is where the universe lies in all of us. We must do the **work** within ourselves to be able to truly make a difference out there. May we all be reminded of the remarkable light beings we truly are.

Life is an intimate act of love between God and ourselves. Because we are God and carry that divinity, it could be seen as Gods' continual act of self-love.

Poetry in Emotion....

Poetry has always held a special place in my heart. The way particular writers can paint a picture and illicit deep waves of emotion with the way they put together the written language was, and is, of deep fascination for me.

When I was in seventh grade we really began to dive into the creative writing process. I was completely enamored! I felt like Merlin casting spells that only I could understand. Expression in motion to which I didn't have to explain.

With the changing of the tides, nothing stays hidden for long, and the glistening shores reveal themselves once more.

We often dismiss our own creativity and uniqueness. We are taught from an early age that to make it in this life we must be better than. Stand out among the masses. If it doesn't speak to the majority then it is irrelevant. If we are unable to paint, sing, photograph, write, (on and on) like those who we would consider The Great's, then it is not good enough. Think about how often you sat in any class learning how to do anything 'like' someone else. Think like this teaching, do like this guy, be like her...

The truth is, these techniques in life that we have been taught, are only a guide at best. Creativity and this immeasurable life encompasses more than what we were taught. Imagination can not be placed in a one size fit's all box. We are not meant to be limited by the examples of others. We all have a uniqueness that is our own and yet we refrain from sharing our own perceptions because we don't feel it is of any worth to anyone but ourselves. This is a fallacy created from fear.

We were created from imagination.

The possibilities and variables are endless. If one believes we are sparks of that infinite source, then why would we ever believe that our own inherent thoughts and visions are of any less value?

Often these are lessons in bravery. To willingly show to the world around us a glimpse of our own unique view can be fraught with fear. Fear being the acceptance of others. This in turn becomes a lesson in non-judgement and a lesson in acceptance and love. And so, the wheel turns.

Knowing this has forced me to practice what I preach. I believe in leading by example (though I am not always successful) for this is how we will change the world.

So here I write and compile these glimpses of me. The inner workings of my essence, in hope that it will encourage my family to 'BE THEMSELVES'. Let the paint lead your art. Allow the words to bounce across the page. Let your feet guide your walk. You never know who you will inspire. How many seeds will be caught in the wind and spread out like ripples in the water. We are never more effective and inspiring than when we are authentically ourselves.

Suits of Power

Often, we hand over our power to others. -- Our parents, our friends, our society. We hang on to a story largely built on another's opinion of us. What we 'should' be doing. Who we 'should' be. Where we 'should' be. We willingly take on these packages without bothering to see where they are coming from.

When we feel slighted, belittled or disrespected we automatically blame another. In that moment we have willingly handed over the guidance system for our own vessel. But, we can regain control of our ship! By doing the internal work and asking the hard questions about these packages, we can transcend the public transportation we have so expertly ridden. We often convince ourselves that we don't want to see what we are reflecting. When looking in the mirror, we quickly fall into the line of self judgment. With a little tweaking of perception, we can learn to go beyond self judgement. It then becomes much like having to walk through the spiders' web to reach Eden! An adventure sprinkled with fear and bound by fortitude! How much do we truly yearn for that space of self acceptance, and how bravely can we nurture ourselves to get there?

Like the representation of the onion. Layers upon layers. The deeper we go, the closer to the heart we get.

How do we do this?

We take a moment.

We begin to settle, to breathe and begin to ask the questions.

Why did that make me upset?

It made me feel bad, small and insignificant.

Why did it make me feel small and insignificant?

Because I have always been made to feel that way when I step forward.

Why have I always felt that way?

Any time I would share my thoughts I was always told I didn't know anything.

Why do I think I don't know anything?

Because that's what everyone has told me.

So, I feel you don't know anything because 'others' told me so?

Yes.

In my heart did my thoughts make sense to me?

Yes.

So, then I have assumed others know my own genius better than I do and I am looking for validation and acceptance?

At the end of the day, we have taken on the opinions and insecurities of others. We learn to ignore our own heart, constantly searching for a place to fit in. We learn to play small and insignificant within ourselves and our world. We turn to the outside to gain recognition for which we can not sustain. Forgetting that our own heart and skin is the only place we need to fit in.

We long for approval and apology from outside forces. Should it arrive, we are still left feeling empty, for no one can truly know our individual heart. True understanding, as we imagine it to be, is futile. A true sense of commonality at this level lies only in our imagination.

We need to venture one step further to fully take the wheel of our own vessel. It is a surrendering to ourselves. At the core, beyond all training and blind belief, we ourselves feel insignificant and small. We have allowed this to radiate out like a beacon beckoning to prove us right in our own view of ourselves. Due to our own lack of self respect and self love we have unwittingly set ourselves up to receive only that which validates our own lack of self worth.

It is a lone journey, this life. The journey to the self can carry no company.

Cultures all over the world have shown us the importance of the self. Journeying, soul retrievals, meditations and prayer to name a few, are all tools to reconnect to our own divinity. Find and love the unique being you are so we too may see and stand in awe!

As Lady Galadriel says to Frodo, "To bear a ring of power is to be alone."

We all bear a ring of power, only ours comes as a suit which is our vessel. Bearing our Suits of Power we are alone. A suit made of flesh, blood and bone. No one can truly understand our suit for it has room for only one.

That is where the beauty lies. A gift beyond all measure. Though we are alone in this gift, so is all others upon this Earth. Each one only responsible to wear and care for their own Suits of Power as we all travel along a path of our own choosing. It is what we all share. The responsibility of loving and honoring ourselves lies *within* ourselves. Each of us holds a heart that only speaks to us, in a language that only we can understand. A guidance system only we can truly operate.

That is where true communion lies. All of us individual drops in the ocean of life. Together individually bound by our suits. We are all fragments of divinity, riding and navigating in our own unique suits.

I have accepted and surrendered to that knowledge. Becoming, essentially, my own best friend and holding my own hand. Accepting the nourishment of others, graciously and contemplative.

Together, we make the human experience.

Together, life.

Remembrance

Whispers of a time long since past
tantalize my mind, my heart.
It is a yearning for something seemingly forgotten.
A memory of a language formed before words,
connection with elements between visible worlds.
Mesmerizing rains tickling my frame,
the serene scents racing through my nose.
Where trees enveloped me so to tell the sun to share,
and the moisture filled ground soothes my familiar toes.
Seduction plays at my senses,
your fragrance a warm hug into my soul.
A time where the only light shed in the dark of night
was the moon and her starlets kissing our eyes.
No more do we venture for the art and communion.
Each day brings forth another vehicle of separation
where we are blinded by the self and fear the breathing.

Oh, how I weep.

Each dawn brings forth another way to silence you.
Waves of malcontent wash over your dying shores.
Feet pound upon your body,
wrapped so you may not know their energy,
and they may not know yours.
Parts of your body bludgeoned for your life,
while other spaces of skin are no more than a brief
destination.
Tears now replace what once was your dancing rain,
The conjured scents now pulverize me,
blinding me to what once was the sweet of you.
Vision is only obtained beneath the shackles of bulbs,
and disparity and numbness are the barges to obtain.
Whisper again, so I may feel your breath press
against my neck.

Guide me to heal upon your breast,
for not all is lost to the ravages of this existence.
Mmmm...my heart awakens,
The kiss.

My sight returns to your skin, your pulse.
The tender soles of my feet, enamored by your love,
remembering the conversation of a time past.
One I am, lost in the jungle of obscurity and disconnect,
but One I AM.

Each fresh kiss of the sun sheds a new tremor of hope.
More press their hearts to remember you,
timid though they may be.
Reminiscent of the first song,
in a place where words are irrelevant, and the
spirit endures,
I join you here.

To Be Nature

Hmmm...Nature.

Beautiful, ecstatic, healing.

When we think of nature what comes to mind? Is it the serene scenes of a forest after a gentle rain? A coral reef teaming with colour? Perhaps it's the meadow alive with flowers and bees buzzing away in your heart.

I think of all those and more. Nature feeds and heals us in ways that words will never be able to convey, but Nature is not just these things. Nature includes people.

Humanity, individual people, are fascinating. All so very different yet so very much the same.

There isn't a day that goes by that I don't learn something new about someone. Maybe I have met someone new. More often than not I learn and see something about someone I have known for a while. Usually it's something I hadn't been aware of before. A glimmer into how they look at things, how they process. Sometimes it is because they are transforming in their lives. Usually it is because I am growing in mine.

As many different people there are on this planet is the many different views, processes, Aha's, and complexities there are. Absolutely no two people think and feel exactly the same. Similar maybe, but never the same.

WOW!

I find the more I allow myself to be more open, more of an observer, the more I am able to widen my views and the better I am to see people clearer. -- To hear what is being said between the words.

We really are no different than the community of trees, birds, and animals. We find strength together. On one side we, together like a colony of ants, can achieve greatness. Building up our homes and providing our nourishment.

That is great, but many of us relish in independence. We are not looking for conformity in a community. We are not ants. Unfortunately, we say we cherish diversity, however the wolf that leaves the pack for their own calling, is often ridiculed and cut out altogether. Left to fend for itself.

When I observe people, one thing I often pick up is how we want to be part of a community, but we want to feel free to express ourselves too. We feel pressure, however, to conform. Pressure from ourselves as much as from the community we think we are in.

The fear of being ridiculed and shut out keeps us from flowering. What we don't like to see is how in turn we do that very thing to others who are also trying to bloom.

Chances are it is fear. Comfort comes in hiding within a crowd. Fear. Fear of not being good enough, smart enough, individual enough or simply enough.

Humans. The only animal in nature, that I can think of, that is fear based.

Fascinating!

There are times I conform to the fear and choose not to speak my truth as I see it so I don't have to face the ridicule, the side ways glances, the sarcastic questions. More and more however, I find I am not concerned with those fears anymore, because in the end they are simply how *I* see things. Nothing else.

I look out into nature and see the occasional lone tree, out there on their own. Daring the elements. Forests are marvelous, but the thing that will always grab my attention is the tree outside of the tree line. The flower that sprouted in the concrete.

The more I observe the actions and reactions of people the more I am seeing and hearing a shift. A movement towards community that is not conformity based, but individual based. Slowly these lone trees are growing together with diversity and flourishing in a way that no other fear-based community can achieve. Evolving like the forest -- full of different species, different flora, different shades of green and brown, all communing in their own way and achieving a quiet strength and endurance.

There are still the spaces that are witheringly close and restricting, but nature is always changing and adapting, and this communal change will, *IS*, taking hold. And to me this is nature at its finest. Symbiosis in action. This makes me feel so infinitely large and so infinitesimally small all at the same time. This is where I focus my attention. Attention to the communal no matter the shape, colour, breed, species or name we give it. Attention to the love that is everywhere in nature.

In us.

Because we are nature too.

In our effort to hold ourselves in high regard.

Prove that we are sentient and intelligent,

we have forgotten our fundamental state of being.

Connection.

Separation is a figment of our limited minds.

Coming - Unity

Community

How can we feel community?

How do you feel something when you are unsure about what it truly means?

We don't know our neighbors.

We don't hang with those circles.

We don't 'agree' with their views, how they live, and what they do.

We don't want to be like them, and we don't think like them.

How can we feel community in a community where we don't KNOW each other?

Easy.

You look inside.

Unity does not mean Uniformity.

You see the community that lives inside you,

Those beautiful cells are not the same.

They don't care what your name is, what you do for a living or what colour you paint your toes.

They do not concern themselves with the Who, What, Whens and Wheres.

They each have their own strengths and functions.

They do not worry about being a skin cell when they are a liver cell.

They are working towards a commonality.

They have a vision of a most wondrous picture.

The most amazing sight you will ever see!

YOU!

See now?

You don't have to FEEL community....YOU ARE COMMUNITY!!!

Coming-Unity

Furthering Coming - Unity

Each moment is a reflection of what we create within ourselves. Every thought. Every action. Every emotion. Within each of us is a community of our own creation responding to the love, or lack of love, that we send.

Each of us is looking for a place to belong. To fit in. To find a place to be our authentic selves yet, every time we send judgment outward we are also sending it in inwards. We disempower ourselves and those around us by radiating outwards our own inner misconceptions.

Choosing to view and feed our inner sanctum bowls of love and compassion, sets in motion a new reality within us. A new, more inviting and complete community of our preference. We move out of the inner city of chaos to a more open, involved and evolved expanse limited only by our own beliefs.

Community begins within ourselves. Recreating these bonds are essential.

We are deserving of our own love and compassion. By loving ourselves and all that come together to make us who we are, we are then allowing our light to shine through. We now see that our universal cup is forever filling. Overflowing!

Each person creating their own inner neighbourhood. Each person sharing in a journey of life that is unique.

That is where the bonds lie. Acceptance of one another and our beautiful way of interacting with ourselves and each other. We are then able to open our eyes to that which are the communities around us. All of these pull us closer to all we are trying to cease.

It is taking the hand of angst, contempt, anger and all that we don't want to feel, and looking deep into the depths that will free us. A graciousness to know that these are all children of our own making that we can love into partnerships. A dance evolution of teacher to student to teacher to student. Embracing the infinity of this cycle. To know that each revolution brings us closer still to what we've allowed our ego to deny. It is the running away that creates the suffering. The egoic thoughts that say fear must be concurred and abolished. The blaming and hiding from ourselves that creates division. Life is a series of ripples set forth by the frequencies we throw and it begins with the vibrations we radiate inward. We hold, within ourselves, a nation of universal proportions. Every cell within in us has come to us, by us. Each one our own solar system brought together to make the universe that is US. The multiverse that is We. The Omniverse that is ever present. Our true essence. Creation creating and recreating itself into itself.

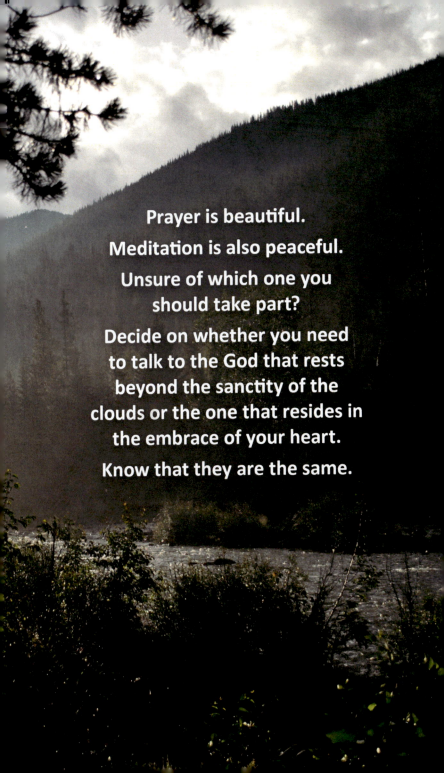

FEAR

Fear of judgement often leads us to hand the reigns of our own lives over to someone else. Convinced that we don't truly know what is in our own heart has left us continually handing over our power, happiness, and love. What we are often left with is a never-ending cycle of 'Shoulds'. We turn away from our own guidance system and blindly bow and follow the 'masses'. As a result, we have succumbed to an existence devoid of honest communion and life. We tirelessly trudge on from one empty promise to another weighted and unfulfilled.

Fear is a never-ending struggle with ego. Continuously we conjure stories to keep us embedded in an element of delusional control. We fight fervently to hang onto feelings of bliss or our normalcy. In this push-pull dance, what we are actually doing is yanking ourselves further from our full potential. Our own Bliss.

Fear keeps us locked in a state of doing. Everything in our daily lives becomes a distraction so we don't have to face what we ourselves have created. Yes, we have created our own fears by the element of imagination. Strengthening it with copious amounts of 'validation' from past perceptions and well-meaning advice laced with...you guessed it! More fear!

How do we move past these monsters of our own creation?

Where do we start?

Look in the mirror. I know. No one wants to admit their own short comings.

As I looked further into the roots of my own monsters, I found it came to my own perceptions during those pivotal times. Neither right nor wrong, merely the way I managed to view things. In away it helped me "get by".

What we resist, persists, where our attention goes, grows.

Where you place your focus is one of the most powerful tools you have. The moment I could begin to speak to myself and view myself as one of my children, there was a shift. I have worked hard to give my own children the love and understanding I didn't feel as a child. Why wasn't I doing that for myself?

So, I began to look at those monsters in the closet as lessons. That is what they are in the end. Lessons we have signed up for before we took our first breath into this life. Even when I couldn't release them, I could at least start liking them, even loving them.

It is fascinating to look back and see the growth that comes from small miniscule steps taken over time. The imagery of what seems like lifetimes, scroll through my mind like an old movie. The knowledge that each of these timid steps, and even the large leaps of faith, have brought is immeasurable. Though many would chalk it up to bravery and resilience could be seen as true. I don't look at it as such really.

Yes, it does take a level of courage to face the monsters in the dark but, more so, it takes love. Love and compassion for the journey you have chosen to create. Perhaps it is knowing that we have the power to create whatever experience we want, that has left me a wee bit braver but, I feel that it is a more the knowing that Love is the binding force of all that is. I see Love in the center of the wheel and everything is simply the spokes extending out. The further from the center, the further from Love. All those emotions and actions that seem quite opposite of Love, can now be seen at the core as Love, albeit distorted, still Love. It is the driving force of all that is manifested.

Even fear, for it is fear that keeps us safe in many ways. The love of self preservation inevitably creates our fear.

Life, I believe, gives us what we need, when we need it. I spent the majority of my younger years locked in a bubble fear. Seemed as though each time I would step out I would be left with shame and revert back into my bubble.

It was those minor experiences that kept me contained.

Those were the experiences I had until I began to look inward and slowly work through one of my missions here. Lack of self esteem and confidence has been a recurring theme, yet at the same time experiences also came that would show me I was capable of learning and moving beyond. Every instance of fear and shame was also met with an invitation to grow. Life giving me what I need, all I had to do was recognize it and grab hold.

Balance. All things in balance.

The more I dared to look fear in the eye and make it a less intimidating friend, I found the more I could embrace my heart and mind for the unique perspectives it has afforded me. When I had first started my little blog, I had no idea the personal growth and freedom that was to come. It became my tool to expand and explore. I am more than a passing thought of existence, and life has become more magical than I could have ever imagined!

Garden Of Fears

*As I walk through the Garden of Fears,
mildew and mold cling to my feet.*

Dank.

Dark.

Lonely.

*Darker still are the remnants of leaves, once
vibrant with life,
now pressed to the earth sticky with regret.*

*As I walk through the rows, my feet become cold with
'should haves',
My hands drip with 'not enough'
and all the while my heart shivers with emptiness.*

But that is only a season...

*For this garden,
This Garden!
Is in rejuvenation!*

As all decay must first appear as dank and foreboding.

*Just below the surface is a sheltered warmth,
A light.
Swimming below is birth, a newness of life.*

*For the dark becomes comfort.
Dank is only needed moisture.*

Lonely is simply reflection.

Reflection of light and the inner knowing.

As each seed bursts forth, we hold hands.

Eyes become clear to the process of energy transformation.
All is temporary and necessary.

Welcome to my Garden of Flowers!

Every spark, a purpose.
Every shadow a mere break from the heat of life.

Necessary.

United.

Here not every laughter needs to be heard,
nor does every tear need to be wiped.

All blooms and decays in perfect symbolism, synchronization.

Growth is nurtured and uninhibited by the falsities of ego.

Welcome to MY Garden.

Feel

Feel everything. The sorrow, the anger, the passion, the love, the joy and everything in between.

When we allow ourselves to feel, when we allow those first waves of rawness, of momentary truth,
then, and only then, are we able to understand.
Understand that person, that situation, you.
Not with our intellectual brain, but with our souls. Our divine selves.
That place beyond the language of words. The place where true knowledge lies beckoning us to remember.

Remember, that amidst all the coverings of a three dimensional world, we come from a place where emotions are simply another energy wave waiting to be experienced. Like a ride at the carnival.
Experiential and enticing.
Free from the imaginations and limitations of our mind.
Our egoic judgement.
Flowing within us, through us, and of us.

Love is the minute particles of magic that hold space and time together. It gives order where there perceives to be none, and light when there seems only darkness.

Move Me

Movement, in any form, is blissful. It allows you to fly above yourself, be yourself, with yourself.

Have you ever looked up and watched moths or butterflies flutter around? It looks so helter-skelter, especially when there are two or more of them. This random unchoreographed performance is where it appears. They seem to not have a clue on what they are doing, or where they are going, or who is watching. They flutter around a center that we can't see.

It is beautiful.

Most people think of movement in the physical sense of the word, but as we become more aware we find that progress exists on all levels. Our mental, spiritual and emotional states are in constant motion. The ground where we stand is in perpetual flow. Nothing remains the same. We flutter continually around a center that we can not envision with our physical eyes. It is only when we deny the mobility of heart and soul that one becomes caught in a loop of stagnation. It is the relinquishing ourselves to a landscape before us that creates the magic. Aware of the slopes, edges, and puddles then consciously navigating with them that enhances the dance. When we try to force the evolution, we fall prey to indirection and miss what the experiential landscape has to offer.

Movement on an emotional and spiritual level with no choreography, no right or wrong, no specific destination becomes the flight of the butterfly. Fluttering around an invisible center and enjoying the grace of it in its uncensored state. Surrendering to a breath of wind that can not be seen, only felt.

Flying above myself. Being myself. With myself.

Everything is at it Seems

*Just when you may think everything is desolate and foreboding, like a frozen terrain in throws of winter, you may think that nothing is as it seems.
Just remember, under that expanse of winter wonder lays a world teaming with life merely awaiting the thawing warmth of the sun.
Kind of like us...quietly gathering under the cover of sleep awaiting for that light to come forth and shine through!
Seems to me that Everything is as it seems...*

~*~

*We must learn to push past our fear and Love all our dark,
for it is only in the depths of our own darkness can we arise to see the new dawn.*

~*~

Sand Dunes

I visited down my body's distant rocky shore,
Across the sand dunes of time and the oceans of space.
The rains opened to free the shadows hidden,
A crack in the crust, barely visible, set forth dreams.
The innocence rose bloomed in echoes. How beautiful her voice.
So majestic the breaths of change, a silken touch
Lemon yellow careens to light the soul
A peaceful lens to show the way
Now more sand than rocks touch my feet.

Gratitude is always the beginning

Each of us face uncertainty. Cold and pressing life seems to bombard us with shadows to hide our dreams and make our paths unclear but, in the quietness of our hearts, lies an iridescent ball of light. Pink with gratitude awaiting our arrival. It is here that we are able to see that past the shadows there holds a small white flower. Knowledge, begging to be spoken, and wisdom awaiting to be heard.

Every dark night holds a glimmer of light if only we should allow ourselves to step into the space of grace and open the shades.

It unfolds with Graciousness. An honoring for this path we have chosen and a knowledge that we can always elect to change our course. Gratitude for the answers that will come, but often not in ways that we are expecting. Gratitude turns what seems to be an endless barren landscape, into a meadow of promise brimming with endless possibilities.

All this is available within our own hearts. In our own ball of recognition. For when we are able to shift our focus for even a moment, away from ourselves, Gratitude will then illuminate the way and allow the waters of appreciation to surround us and take us to the ocean of endless sunrises.

Every mind made trial brings with it a lesson nodding in the breeze, a promise of something brighter, and a warm place in which to shelter us.

Gratitude is always the beginning.

Gratitude is always the book in where to find the answers.

So, I took a stroll down the road of normalcy once. It wasn't long before I found it lacked scenery, character and life. I quietly put on my rose-coloured glasses and headed back to bliss where I laid back on my Milky Way hammock, sipped a tall glass of rainbow, and gazed at a beautiful love rise.

Gratitude

Gratitude starts with ourselves. A simple acknowledgement of life. Like everything on this journey, it is an inside job and it starts with each one of us.

Gratitude is more than a word. It is a feeling, a knowing.

Knowing I could have been anyone, anywhere, with any combination of souls to travel with is awe inspiring! But I got to be me!

I had the blessing to have the parents and childhood that gave me the lessons and experiences that helped me evolve to the person I am today. Each moment, each circumstance and every choice I made led me here. Right now, this moment. Though there are junctures in which I can honestly say, I was not proud, gracious, or even understanding, each instance was merely a lesson of grace. Through the rivers of time I have been learning and evolving in the gift of life with gratitude.

Gratitude starts with me.

Grateful for this body that I inhabit. Though there are places I have felt less than gracious for this life vessel, the more I have learned to appreciate it, the more symbiotic we become.

Indebted for this Heart. A Heart with its own voice and wisdom. My beautiful Heart that has shown me, that although I may not like a person, place, situation or even myself, even though it aches and gives me a sense of emptiness, my Heart still loves. Loves each person, place, situation and me. Unconditional.

Gratitude for my mind. A mind that has shown me a different view. A different perspective. Though it hasn't always been easy to hear a different set of drums, it has afforded me a uniquely beautiful symphony, and the more

I see it that way the more my centers work together. Each one slowly vibrating at the same frequency. Forming an unshakable whole.

In the end there is always benediction for Spirit/Creator. For I carry with me always, the knowledge

I am but a seed of the Universe from which all this is possible.

My path is often hidden from view, but if there is one single purpose I should choose to acknowledge, it would be to be able to show each and every being that they too deserve to feel gratitude for themselves. That each should know that they too are so much more than they think. That against all that we have been told to believe, Gratitude is not for a select few, for the more deserving. It is our right. It is the front door to our 'home'. May we all know that we are more courageous, infinitely wiser and wildly more gifted than we 'choose' to see. Should Gratitude of ourselves be our top priority, then what a brighter world we will have gifted ourselves.

Where We all Go

There is a place we all go that is beyond the confines of molecules, beyond where thoughts formulate words. Far beyond the feeling of feelings.

Yes.

Here, where the everything is nothing and nothing is everything.

We gather.

Where moments are evaporated bubbles on a screen. We commune.

Where peace is what is. No thoughts, no emotions, just observers awaiting their turn to congregate amongst the stars like seeds waiting for the wind to set them onward to a new start...a new way of being.

We all go there.

Where silence is all there is.

The cosmos is merely reflections of ourselves and we reflect the cosmos.

We all go there.

To a place that is so familiar it seems strange, but we careen into its' bosom none the less. We long for its embrace to rescue us from ourselves.

Not too soon Love.

Experiences are waiting, needed.

Not too soon Love.

Mysteries are waiting to mystify, electrify.

Not too soon Love.

We need to inspire, conspire, light on fire the world within the world.

Not too soon Love.
We will all go back there....here.
Where our ancestors are our descendants and we are all.
Shhhh...
You are already here Love.
We all are.

The Sun Will Rise

As the sun will continue to rise at dawn each morning,
Our spirits will continue to sing.
Our hearts will continue to speak.
Our guides will continue to show us the way.
Our energy will continue to dance
and,
if we are willing,
we will listen

Life

Life is experience.
An event in a moment of time,
molded from a love incomprehensible to mortal consciousness.
Never the less it is here. We are here. Love is here.
To experience it in all its' colour,
on every strand of cosmic paths and directions.
Life is Love in motion.
Experiencing all in every way possible.
We need only to recognize this and then flow willingly to its' understanding depths.
Love never divides.
It is only our Ego trying to formulate a hold in a world free from restrictions,
that tries desperately to find flaw and imperfections.
Life is conjured by Love.
Free, unrestricted and bountiful Love will take you to places you forgot existed.
Experience
Life
Love

Honor

*If I could reach my hand into all that is,
I would be reaching for you.
If I could summon forces that nothing can hold,
I would be holding you.
If I could stare into the eyes of God,
I would see you.*

Know that in every light and shadow we communicate. Sometimes I talk and you listen. Sometimes you talk and I listen, but always we dance in perfect rhythm.

See beyond the claimed righteousness that many impose and listen to our heart, for that is where our communication resides. They cannot tell you the path that you must take, the choices that you need to make. Only WE, together, know what we must do.

*Free from the confines of the finite, you will flourish.
WE will flourish.*

You are the power and the infinite we have all come to worship.

You are the savior that we have all come to see. Our hopes, fears, loves, and hearts all lie with you.

*You are the magic of the earth and the wisdom of the universe wrapped up so divinely in exquisite uniqueness.
You are the dream and the reality.
You are the pleasure and the pain.
A universe in the multiverse.
You.
You....
You are all that is, that ever will be, that ever was.
You are the collective.*

Each a treasured and valued piece of honor

Whole
Perfect
One.

~*~

No being is better or less than another. We are merely on different journeys for the collective experience. In appreciating this we are then able to let go of the feeling of being less than or more than, or having more or less than another. We begin to appreciate all the ways we are able to experience.

~*~

It's a Matter of Choice

Childhood is rarely an easy step into this world. Fraught with finding my place within my home, school, world and myself, I found myself quite often having conversations with myself. In many ways, it was a way to deal with hardships and what I would perceive as injustices. In the world of my mind I could see everything from a broader perspective. I could escape the physicality of the world and try to process and digest. People watching became, and still is, one of my favorite past times. Growing up in a time free from smart phones and tablets as distractions, I could submerge myself into a world of wondering and noticing. Fascinated by the myriad of ways people chose to interact, react, and respond to the happenings around them. It has been, and continues to be, my greatest teacher of reflection. Not only could I observe my surroundings, but I would learn to become my own best friend and worst enemy.

Why do we make the choices that we do?

Why do some of us feel we don't have a choice? What makes us choose to be compliant, or a rule breaker? Why do we choose to see things as hopeless and this one sees it as opportunity? Why did I choose to go against the grain? When the world said I had every right to play the victim, why did I feel I needed to roll up my sleeves and flex my muscles of defiance? These were but a small fraction of the fuel for the conversations in my head. Enter in the realization of options.

In the end, should there be one, everything comes down to the everyday realizations that we make. Even though we have been adequately trained to place a right or wrong to each decision and action, there really is no right or wrong. There are only the experiences that you are meant to have. We have free will to decide for ourselves whether to run and hide or face life head on. Whether we want to embrace that in which we have been given or to turn from it. Always there is the choice, so if we wish to herd and follow like sheep or forge our own path, that is our own **personal** preference free from the confining labes of right or wrong.

Each decision we make, each choice only adds to the web of life, the collective weaving of something far too expansive to even grasp, though it is a lovely contemplation. Even these thoughts can be dismissed or embraced or expanded upon. It is of no consequence to myself. As I had heard years ago, 'Nothing has meaning until you give it meaning'.

I suppose that is with anything. Love, Life, creation. Find it full of meaning and so it is, find it is a pile of excrement and meaningless, so it is as well. I do hope however, that you will at least find **yourself** full of meaning, but that is also your inherent right, because it becomes a matter of what you believe in!! Whether I am on the mark or off my rocker, I still feel that life on this plane of existence is about the experience. The experience to know who You are and to rejoice in who Everyone else is...whether we accept it or not.

I find I love it.

Choices.

They shape our experience. These experiences collect to form a cohesion of one thoughtful experience to be played and expanded over and over again in a multitude of different ways. No two practices are the same for no set of choices are the same. It is beautifully symbiotic, colourful and monochromatic all at once.

It then becomes ridiculous to think that Awakening should all look identical. Awakening is a journey of SELF discovery. A discovery of the paradoxical - We are individual - We are one.

We know this and yet due to our fabulous individuality we search and wander to explore a space that resides within us. But there again are the choices. No right or wrong, just ideas to add to a collective experience. Another chapter to add to the library of life.

What ever the discretion, the goal is the same - To Awaken.

There is no set rule, belief, study, lifestyle to determine whether you Awaken or not, it is simply by the choices YOU propose to make and when you get there you will know.

How?

Well it will be so ridiculously plain and so ordinary that we are left with what I like to call a "Duh" moment. Now I am not saying that the workings of the universe are simple, nor am I saying that it's not. It is so intrinsically complicated AND simple that it lends itself to an oxymoron. Complicated in the that the variables are endless. No two people will ever have the exact same experience (choices) or the same point of Awakening no matter the similarities of their paths. Simple in that the end result of Awakening is the same. Complete connectedness. Nothing to do, say, feel, or be -- just nothing -- which of course is everything!

Allowing a knowingness that says we are free to reach and stretch for the answers in whatever fashion suits us, but it also says we already have them...not all of them of course, just a drop.

Awakening is now.

Does this lend to say that there aren't lessons around the corner or new discoveries? Not at all, there is just a freedom of peace that accompanies them. It is all still very necessary. One firing neuron in the brain is no less instrumental in the shaping of the infinite as one exploding star in space.

Every decision is exactly that, a choice. No right or wrong, no judgement. It all adds to the garden of life that is watered by the wonder of the universe.

Miraculously Simple, Ordinarily Complicated.

~*~

Bravery to me is stepping away from our self-imposed boxes. The ones we create every time we take on the beliefs of society, family, friends. In the end it is not these beliefs per say, but the way we have individually perceived them and ultimately created within ourselves.

Valor is simply peeking past our own blinders that we have set in place. Seeing ourselves as the creators of our lives and choosing to continue or create something else.

These moments of fearlessness happen within ourselves all the time. It is setting aside the mind and emotions to allow our Soul to lead. It is our Soul that knows, and our body and mind that we are trying to convince of our inherent uniqueness and divinity. It is not so much a crushing of fear and all those shadows that arise but taking them by the hand and honoring them as a teacher, and now showing them the light of the student. The light that unfolds with every blessed step taken, and every one not taken. It is no less valiant keeping ones self confined than it is to change. Courage is being okay to be where you are right now. It is as individualistic as the being.

Bravery is listening to your own Soul.

Each moment in our lives we are reflections of one another. No more. No less. All perfect adaptations of a universe in motion. Whether we choose to hide, or embrace, life is here awaiting our willingness to adapt and evolve. The unknown becomes a place of wonder as opposed to fear. Curiosity of what it is we can be, we will be, and what we are.

Shadows become nothing more than a reprieve from the light. A space in which we can better see and appreciate the ever glow of a sun that will forever shine upon our highest potential. As the seasons change and adapt to the wisdom of our Earth and the universe before us, so we must as well. Accept each as a growth of opportunity and a release from the mundane. Gone be the moments spent in fear and contempt, judgement and self loathing. Welcome the solace of a journey spent looking into your own essence that resides in the souls of all that you come in contact with, for it is in that space that fear can not be.

And so, it is.

Change no longer something to angst, but an evolution to be honored. Each wave passing lovingly upon the sands of time. Tickling each granule with wonder, curiosity and love. Nurtured, supported and recognized.

Cradled close in the bosom of Mother Earth and held tight by the arms of the Universe.

What makes me gaze upon the mystery of a night sky, or ponder the steady meandering of an ample stream?

I imagine it comes down to wondering how I fit in to this vast universe. I feel we are in a perpetual search to find our place. Some looking for a connection to the heavens and others for a connection to this earth and most looking to find themselves in each other. Myself? It encompasses all of these and more. Life, for me, is a continual classroom filled with more questions as answers to my questions. In a society built on looking for definitive answers, stored in appropriate boxes, one can be left in a field of frustration and agony. Being left out in the open air of trust, without seeing the answers, can feel too daunting, too full of fear and demons. Ultimately, we seek a branch to hold fast to, lest we be carried off on an unforeseen adventure. We forget that this whole excursion has no predetermined stops, other than the ones WE create.

Imagine

Imagine I will.
The expansiveness of life,
cosmic relations brought through me.
Dream I did.
Hearts openness to fire,
minds widen to rivers flowing.
Imagine I will.
Space unfolding, a new page turning,
truth is spoken beyond the silence.
Dream I did.
Captive audience transcending lies,
subjects teaming for new.
Imagine I will.
New eyes widening to tears unshed,
A chorus of songs melodious
Dream I did.
Wonders remaining to feel,
magic is at our fingertips.
Imagine I will.
Breath beyond body,
movement in unreality.
Yesterdays' dreams.
Tomorrows' imagines.
Today I will.

What have you done for yourself

When was the last time you did something for yourself?

Are you thinking that you have just had a spa day, a night out with the girls, maybe you have a shopping day planned or you are finally getting an extra hour of some much-needed sleep? Are you thinking of a time you paid it forward or dished out some good advice for once? Perhaps you feel going to the gym, buying those great shoes or managing the last piece of pie before the kids got to it, is plenty.

Whatever the venue, they are all great and we need to be free to explore these means that interest us, for they all can be momentarily gratifying.

What I am asking is; When was the last time you did something for *Your-Self*? When was the last time you allowed the anger that rages through your veins bubble forth and scream to heavens until at last it was nothing more than a lonely leaf careening off in the distance? When was the last time you gave your *Self* permission to wail in frustration and sorrow until the last tethered tear rendered itself free from its prison of perceived control? Have you let your *Self*, even for a moment, delve into the abyss of hopelessness? Have you allowed those feelings to summon forth complete and utter helplessness and loneliness until you are nothing more than a trembling mass melded to the coming dark?

There is always the other side that we are afraid to let free as well. Why would we let our *Self* be too happy and contagious? That will only allow us to fall deeper when the shadows peek around to pull us down to reality. Isn't that what we think we are doing when we try and 'contain' our *Self*? Protecting it, sheltering it so it may not hurt too much, see too much, be disappointed too much. In the end all we have really done is let our *Self* down. We came in promising our *Self* the world of experience, however that may turn out, and instead we became a resentful parent trying to catch a moment of solace with a handful of empty promises we are too frightened to keep. Our *Self* needs, craves those moments of deep experience. Our *Self* has no concept of social decorum, no agenda for linear rights or wrongs. It is only committed to flowing forth to touch what our physical eyes are unwilling to see and our mortal minds refuse to acknowledge.

Our *Self* is in an undaunting search to release from our containment and simply be. Yet we hold fast to our seemingly protective nature to control and in the end, we do our *Self* the worst kind of indignation. Smothering layers of useless contaminants to silence the roar much like we would a child. Giving into the distractions that is said to bring happiness instead of summoning up the courage to simply sit and listen ... and do nothing...and just be...and truly feel the absoluteness of our *Self*.

To know how perfect everything is. Not dark, not light, just being an observer and experiencer under one conscience.

So, I ask you again, what have you done for your *Self* lately?

A Deep Breath

A beautiful tribe of women entranced by a magical ride called Nia, inspired this interlude. At a time when I desperately needed to be freed from the confines of my mind, the universe blessed me with Lise and her tribe of amazing Love warriors, for which I am eternally grateful. Ladies, this is for you.

Early Evening, it is time.
The body begins to awaken
reaching, stretching for the I am.
Acknowledging the heavens.
Touching heart.
The Love is awakened.
Bow to the earth.
I feel You.
Above, Centre, Below,
the I LOVE YOU in form.
It starts a whisper beckoning.
The dream begins to play.
Soft caresses within the ear.
This is for Us.
Mesmerizing hope,
a longing deep inside.
A burst of colour radiates.
The lights fall and the shadows disappear.
The body no longer tied to time.
Magic descends, Love flows forth
and she sings...and She SINGS
FREE! FREE!! FREE!!!
A deep breath.......
AAAAHhhhhhhhhhh
A sensuous wisp settles, sending forth the spirit,

the life.
Inspiration abounds, calm, open, abundant,
leaving the soul window open.
Open peace, Open eye, Open love, Open soul
Simply
Breathlessly
Lovely

I AM

I am happy.

The key in this statement is:

I AM.

A simple yet profound statement I AM.

Our innate being is that of joy. The absolute and unrestricted joy of being here in this time on this very planetary plane of existence is who we are. We often refer to someone or something as 'making' us happy or bringing us joy, but the truth is nothing 'brings' us happiness or joy or love. We have unwittingly convinced ourselves that this blissful state of being has been handed to us from something other that what we are. When something or someone 'makes' us happy, it not that they have 'made' us, it is only that they have enhanced within us that which is already there. That piece of us that for one reason or another we have stuffed down to only come out during special occasions, or when appropriate.

To be joyful, gracious, peaceful is a power we all have and it is not needed to be contained. Let it free. It's our right to dispel with anything that is meant to discourage our being. Our True being. Society has been designed to sell versions of bliss and peace, but the truth be told it cannot be bought. You cannot buy the Sun and tell it to rise and set, nor the Moon, so why do we think we are any less?

It is okay to wake up and feel the joy of a sunrise, rainy day, even a great thunder storm! This ideology that we are meant for stress, fear, judgment....is a mediocre attempt to contain us. For some it is all we feel we know. It falls into the 'should' s' of our ancestral coding, but it can be set aside and reset to our original being. Anything else other than that of pure joy has been habitual, and like any habit it merely takes an awareness, then it can be altered, thanked for the lessons it has taught, the experiences it brought, then released back into the wild so we may allow room for our own light to bloom uninhibited and free!!

So, let it go! Freedom can feel scary, but in reality, it sets a level of comfort and security that is simply unachievable by any other means.

I AM happy

I AM joy

I AM peace

I AM a PERFECT creative expression of all that is!

Nothing else is needed, only you.

Thoughtful awareness...

Often, we think that we don't know how to be present and in the moment. Truth is, we have these moments continually. Moments are continual. We are simply unaware of it. Each time we are caught up in that perfect sunrise, a child playing, a book, whatever catches our attention, we are in that moment.

Being present also doesn't mean that it is a fleeting passage of time lasting a mere second or two. It is the elementary state of being immersed in whatever it is we are doing. We become the observer in our own lives. It is observing and executing simultaneously. We only need to bring our awareness to this and bring it forth to our every day. The instant we realize we have been on auto pilot, we have now become aware and in that space. It is our natural state.

Every fragment then becomes a blessing. It is the beginning of mindfulness. Realizing that each has been a lesson and a gift that has brought you to this time. A gift made of universal love to express universal love. The gift that is us.

A Dream

Was it only a dream or perhaps something more?
So much, it would seem, calls us. Beckoning us to something bigger than ourselves.

With each passing day it is hard to see it.

The world of humans, cycled into a spiral of self degradation, feels lost in their mindless creations.

Each moment, a chance to steal the safety of our own being.
Fear, a great motivator. Sheltering us into a box of ill-perceived safety.
This, of course, is where the weak minded want us.

Easily we are swayed and subdued. Fearing the warmth of the Sun and the healing beneath our feet.
We muster forward, or that is what we tell ourselves, but in truth we recoil.
Regress into a conditioned sense of belonging and righteousness.
Divided and lost.
As screens fill our sights, and division seeps into our minds,
we comfort the layers of our existence.
Upon ourselves we hide amongst the production of 'happiness',
burying the hopes and remembrance of something greater.
Misguided and misrepresented,
we fall into conditioning and routine.
Easily we are seduced by false belonging,
false ease.
Replacing the nature of us with physical contortion.

Shall we be destined to be nothing more than an experiential malice, quickly forgotten?
Forever circling the chasms of our fear?
Will this repeater of history, so bound in proving how sentient we are,
be nothing more than a lost page of time floating endlessly through the planes of existence?

Even now, I feel the icy hand creep into my heart.
Chilling the bones of my self.
Darkness, so seductive, clamors for my company.

Perhaps I shall succumb.
Nestle deep into the chaos.
Keep steady and look down.
Follow and conform to a calamity that, though it boasts peace,
will bring me to the chains of despondency and endless desires.

I have felt them, you know.
The comforting weight of them.
Like silk spread upon a bed, inviting and beckoning.
The illusion of satisfaction only a dream away.
A temptress needing me only to allow myself to me swallowed.
Ahhh...but I listen.
Not to the endless wale of division,
the caterwauling of righteousness and blindness.

No, I listen.

Beneath the calamity, behind the smoke of despair,
Can you hear it?
A soft tone, barely audible.
The self.
The self.

Subtle, soft, consistent.
An echo locator for my soul

Whispers, 'Look up. Look up'
And I listen.

My heart raises her head, slow and trembling
What will I see? The fears that taunt me? The chains that tickle my fingers?

'Open your Eye'
So, I listen.

And there, beyond the noise, the sun kisses the horizon.
Dancing it's light upon the clouds.
I can see, surpassing the visions of sight,
exceeding the malice, the endless space,
The light.

A dream?
Perhaps.

But awareness settles into my view.
An endless wonder of self's waking to the call.
Separated, only by the distance created in the mind.
Glimmering stars of hope in the vastness of ourselves.

The icy hand that threatened to take hold,
melts and joins.
Communion no longer a mysterious thought
fraught with ego.
I am awakened to the knowledge that a stormy sky
is only that.
Beneath the dank floor of decomposition, I hear them.

Hope renews on the waves of shadow.
This is all.
Brief flickers of light coalescing into flame.

The nightmare from which I awoke to the dream in which we are.
Unity, not only with one another, no longer a word, but a reality, out stretched by the disadvantages of our eyes.
Pulses of energy.

From a place where language, as we know it, does not exist,
we are birthed.
Into a creation we have contorted,
We will flounder.
In this cataclysm, onward we will forge the remembrance of
creation itself.
Free to encompass, to see, to listen.
To create that in which we dream we are.

Lead by example without expectation.

Lead by your own authenticity of who you are in the moment,

knowing the next moment can hold differently.

Simply Flow

Natural flow is the essence of being.

In attempts to bring forth more meaning much has been lost. Time is spent either defending the illusions of societal control or spent fighting the systematic conformity of this self - serving society. Both sides, unwittingly, resisting the essence, the balance, and the flow.

It is not an all or nothing state of being. It is not conformity and yet it is also not the absence of conformity that brings forth the energetic pulse of life. It is understood that congregation holds a certain amount of comfort for many.

There is no one way. There never has been one way.

Whether one is immersed in a formal religious institution, group, or set of ideals, or running away from any particular construct, one must remember that it is not these in itself that will bring about evolution, but instead it comes from the individual and their uniqueness.

If you were to strip away all the rules and regulations, take away all the ceremony and fluff, let go of what is told to be right or wrong, good or bad, all judgments, what then would be left?

Essence.

The essence of being. Free. Uninhibited and unmediated flow of all that was, could be and is.

A continual swing of cycles. Death and rebirth. An ever - changing scenery allowing a deep knowing of guidance. Directional in only the way the wind can carry us. Picking up what speaks to us, then releasing what doesn't. Understanding that ideals are individualistic and not meant to be a bound set of rules, simply a temporary map in which the direction is completely up to you, like seeds in the wind.

Simply flow.

Know that the connection is always there. Conversations and support is always available, but not always in the way one can expect. Whether the choice is conformity of the masses or a full retreat, know that either way, the direction can never be that black or white. The soul is made to dance in whichever way the wind blows. The art of grasping is that of the physical and it is fear that urges us to confine our being.

Release and know that even butterflies understand that it requires the letting go of one body and stepping into another, a metamorphosis, to BE. Resisting nothing and just surrendering with the changing seasons and floating along to an inner guidance that cannot be defined, but in complete trust of all that is.

Control is an illusion contrived out of fear. Let it go and allow your essence to flow. It will be the most beautiful sight you will ever see.

Today

It is time today to look at the person beside you and understand that they too have a story like you. That they too have perhaps done things in their past, like you, that they wish they didn't. That they too are trying to adjust to a shift that they may or may not understand in their conscious mind. It is time to see them for the beings that they are. Like you they are here for the experience, to grow and remember...Like you they are perfect. It is not your place to judge, but to instead accept that they are on their own path and that in the end you will all find your way. Love will get you there. Understanding will get you there. Patience and allowance will get you there. Your job, as with ours, is to merely allow all that is to do what it is meant to do. Just open your heart space and be. everything is as it should. Trust, allow, and love. Simple.

This Moment

And I woke up this morning to a world full of promise. A sky filled with hope, for the sun has yet to arrive to kiss the earth. She is still asleep, covered with the blanket of slumber, and held by winters magic.

The light grows upon my eyes, and I am always in captivation of what is to come, for I can never be sure of the unfolding.

Should the clouds stay and tantalize me with a promise, or will they wisp away and allow forth the glimmer of warmth that will rain through my windows and sooth the chill still resting on my tired body?

It is never promised, this day that caresses us. Though we would like to believe the morning comes for we have willed it to, the truth is it simply arrives whether we wish it or not.

The birds sing, melodious and sweet.

The sleeping branches sway their winter song.

All creatures bound by this existence continue each morning, each night, as it has always been regardless of my current state of ambiguousness. Each moment in perpetual motion set forth by a hand we can only imagine to be there.

Yes, onward it comes, and I reminded of my minuscule matter in this tidal wave of life. No more than the drop of water careening down the side of my cup, pulled by a force I can not see, but propels me just the same.

Perhaps this is all imagination, fooling myself that I can direct the course my feet should travel. Maybe the destination is no more than words put together to ease my discomfort during times of melancholy. Time no more real than the imaginations of crazy thoughts bought by those still in their dormancy, and willingly scuffed off to those too fraught with confusion to do anything more than follow.

It matters not. The morning will come on a chariot sending forth hues of pink and powdered blue to set the stage. An asseveration of a night that will step aside and ring on the golden disc that is our sun.

Morning, it seems, can not be restrained. Some will greet it dancing, rested on toes bursting with anticipation of a song yet to be heard. Poised for a choreography not yet written, but filled with curiosity and excitement, while others will offer no more recognition to it's statement than that of their discarded thoughts.

And I?

The birds have awakened from their slumber, nattering on about things I can only imagine. The sky has opened and the sun smiles on all that my eyes can feast and beyond. Nothing is certain, and yet, though in the distance there are clouds willing to obscure the light now billowing onto my face, I feel content. Content for now to simply witness the non-discrimination that the winter capped mountains hold as their faces glow with plumes of pink, orange and gold, to hold there until at last their frozen tops lends way to white.

Relaxed to know that regardless of their seeming frivolity flitting about the landscape of prairie and tree, the birds will continue to sing a song I may never understand, but my heart cherishes it just the same.

*Peace. Peace to know that this moment is unlike any moment preceding it, or that will come again. Knowing that in this moment I have captured it as a picture, imprinted on the
pages of my soul, and that each moment proceeding has the purview to extend to such heights and impermanence as this one.*

It is not the words that flow from your lips that speak to my heart, it is the unspoken ones that cascade from the space in between that sing to my soul. May those words always be of the most enchanting melody.

Labels of the Spirit

Belief and Faith.

Most of us think that these two are synonymous. We feel because we believe in a set string of belief systems that it must show faith, or if we implement routine and ceremony that must bring us closer to Source, I Am, God.

For me they are not the same. I feel Faith transcends Belief. Belief gives us a linear, physical way to try and bring us closer to the truth. Beliefs are an attempt to satisfy the mind, comfort our short comings (as we perceive them). Beliefs are designed to make us feel that we must be more dedicated. If we deprive our physical self of certain foods and substances, we must surely be closer to God. If we smudge we must be clear of negative energy. If we follow a set standard of teachings, we must surely be closer to enlightenment. A set of rules in a way.

Beliefs can allow us to put responsibility on some outside force. The paradigm of humanity. Take responsibility for ones' self, but you can rely on...what?... to do it because I have been taught that, or it is tradition?

Faith is not something we do. It is not found in texts, drawings, teachings. It has nothing to do with what we do physically, where we were born, or our lineage. It is not laid out in ceremonies handed down or newly created, in dances, scriptures, or in nature.

Faith lives in our heart. It is an infinite knowing that there is a higher power, consciousness, even though we can not say why we know, it is a feeling that cannot be described; although many have tried. It is not something you can dress up, make more appealing, bend to the control of a select few. It simply just is.

I am not saying beliefs are not necessary to us. Often times we need them if only to find a faith that was there all along. I just find beliefs, when we allow them, can be limiting our individual experiences. How often have you found yourself, or someone else, refusing to entertain an idea because it goes against their beliefs?

Beliefs are often judged because it is out there for all to see, because your beliefs are different than mine.

Our Faith resides within a space that can only, individually, be felt with a side of collective oneness. We believe, individually, that we have the answers (or some of them) we have Faith that in reality, we know nothing, but we are divinely cared for.

We have allowed ourselves to think that attending a practice weekly, is showing our Faith. That deprivation and self-induced suffering shows Faith, worshiping practices and gurus and idols shows Faith.

I Believe in humanity. Humanity can be very inspiring and can create magic when put to the test. I, however, do not have Faith in humanity for it is dependent on individuals who can be less than inspired by their own individual potential for greatness.

I have Faith in the divine order. It cannot be seen or shown. There are no ceremonies. My Faith in the higher consciousness requires nothing more than for me to acknowledge it within my heart.

I Believe in a lot of things and the more I learn and see the more these Beliefs grow to encompass more. Some I am able to let go for they no longer serve. They are in a constant state of expansion. Beliefs can continue to expand, we can them go, or we can allow them to become set and stagnant. What I believe today, will change tomorrow

My Faith, however, is constantly simple. It is an absolute. It is the one thing that regardless of new information, it remains. For me the Faith in a divine consciousness and plan has not wavered regardless of what my mind has learned. It is simple, unexplainable and constant. On a plane of existence, where duality is ever present and is part of the experience, my faith remains the same, but my Beliefs for truth seeking is constantly evolving. I have Faith in something that is far more than we can comprehend on this plane of existence, and it is through this that all else comes.

I don't have Faith because I Believe, I Believe because I have Faith.

Just another Label

Saying I am Spiritual is not devoid of religion, nor is Being Religious mean I lack spirituality. The two hold to each other in a way most are not willing to see. We are so afraid and mistrusting of ourselves. We are insistent that there must only be one way. One path. One divine order.

Religion does that for us. Set us up in a tidy little box with rules and regulations in which we can follow. Spirituality in many ways is regarded as a way to listen to our own inner most truth. It draws on various teachings and insights. It becomes skewed when we humans try to, again as with religion, set in rules. Both paths innately built on the same need to be definitive.

Religion binds rules to religious texts and Spirituality sets outlines based on guru teachings. Those that consider themselves Spiritual often will speak of the multitude of directions we are free to take. Many will then take on the stance of structure. No different than religion. All of it is simply a label in which we try and define ourselves. Then ego sets in and begins to start 'better than, less than' motifs. Both contain truths, but humans love to set in boundaries. We thrive on separation.

In what ever we choose to adhere to, it is all a journey. A journey limited only by our own individual imaginations and constructs.

Oneness

A pondered light
A breath of silence
A myriad of flashes cascade down the path

A thousand stars
An array of darkness
A dimple of colour refreshes the night

A whisper of truth
An honest foray
A tingle of magic stimulates the play

It's beyond the senses
that a soul is revealed

It is beyond emotion
that Love is revered

It's beyond comprehension
that infinity resides

It is beyond contemplation
that Oneness coincides

Good bye Baby Blanket

Thoughts riddled with conformity. Ideas tainted with the pollution of another's' rights or wrongs. How many times have you caught yourself saying;

"That's the way it has always been.''

"So and So said this."

"All the experts say _____ and so it must be".

How many times have you known something didn't feel right? Didn't quite add up, but you went along anyway because you didn't feel formally educated enough? Or perhaps you thought you didn't have the knowledge to argue with those whom have formally studied for decades? I don't discredit formal education. It has a purpose to teach us the fundamentals which are important. What I find disconcerting is that we have placed so much of our faith in it. We have allowed a systematic stripping of our own inner knowledge. The more we buy into it the less inclined we are to think for ourselves. Education then becomes the studying of someone else's interpretation of how things ought to be because it fits in to their view of reality.

Best we herd like sheep than face the wolf.

We are forever seeking. In fact, we refer to ourselves as seekers. Seeking for answers, God, reasons, our purpose, the light, the truth, the one true way. We spend countless hours, years, seeking for the meaning of these seemingly insurmountable mountains. Some say that it is part of the journey. Each individual soul molding and learning itself into divinity, or at least trying to. We convince ourselves that this must be the purpose.

'I know the truth for I have seen it, heard it, been told, taught, felt'.

Perhaps that is so. We have assured ourselves that someone else, whether it be a teacher, preacher, guru, therapist, must have the answers. For some of us that feels true. In the end, we all know the answers that lie hidden in the chasms of our depths, but we don't want to delve in there. Why? Because it is not what or where we want the answers to be. Oh yes, we are seekers, but we seek for a truth that fits our personal agendas. We seek to find what fits into our field of view. Our makeshift reality takes the lead so that we can feel we have some control. As a seeker of sorts, if there is anything I have learned, it would be: That there is no set rule! Nothing for us to physically grab hold of. And that is scary! It lends knowledge to how little control we have. What we thought is supporting us in our quests is nothing more than a weak thread ready to snap free from our grasp. It feels like falling with nothing to grab onto! Like sliding off a tin roof. You're just spiralling down, down, down. Ironically enough if you surrender to the fear and take hold and embrace it, you find that you are not falling at all. Simply gliding through your method of experiences! Adding to your own revolution. I like to refer to it as being an infant. Finally having the courage to let go of table and take those steps. Frightening and freeing all at the same time. No, we don't need to hang onto the prescribed teachings laid before us. Your Soul legs are more than able to carry you. When you let it all go the seeking stops. You find yourself just being. Adding your ingredients to a collective recipe of life. Yes, you're a necessary ingredient! Yes, you make a difference! Yes, it all matters! To what extent? I don't know, but Everything, Everyone, has a purpose. Even in those times we are unwilling to see it.

Not what you wanted to hear?

The truth, as we begin to see it, rarely is. Perhaps that is only a truth I am wanting to see.

The baby gate is down. The room is big and open. The floor, walls, and ceiling have all faded away and I am letting go of one 'supportive' instrument at a time. No longer seeking for something that will fit into this space but floating onward in awe. To experience what comes my way and to see the wonder in it all.

Good bye baby blanket.

Love is the hidden truth of which all is created, it is only the distortion of our illusionary fears that tells us otherwise.

A little Food For Thought

So, is it safe to say then, that it is not so much the absence of thought, but the 'not following' of thought? That this practice is a way to calm the mind and attached emotions (the camouflage) so that we may then hear/feel ourselves (soul/essence) at our trueness? That the soul/our being is already all knowing so essentially all we need to do is clear away the clutter, reconnect and remember, and then reintegrate our true essence with thought and emotion to then become the conscious experience of physical life and that may have been the original intention?

We often say that it is the Soul that needs remembering or reminding. We tell ourselves that it is the Soul that needs to be convinced to forgive, release or love. 'I know it now because it has reached my Soul.' Or 'I know it in my mind, but it is my Soul I needed to convince.'

That is the fallacy that we have conditioned ourselves to believe. Truth be told, it is our physical/mental being that needs to be reminded. It is the egoic mind that needs to be brought back to the level of knowing. The Soul already knows. It is our Soul that gives us that inner knowing. The whisper in the wind. The gentle nudge of where we need to turn. That gut instinct, as we like to call it. You see the Soul is what we already ARE. It is already the knowledge of the ages.

Everything else is the concealment that allows us to experience life without the direct knowing being fully visible. The mind, body, and emotions that we create is essentially how we can move and perceive a physical life of experience. To be able to attach the feelings that come with loss, anger, despair, joy, peace, gratitude, and love, one must come in direct contact with them.

It is a way to take knowledge of something one has already, and now be able to see it move.

Music is already music, but we won't know how the notes written on the page will sound and feel until we actually *play* it. Experience, to add to the knowledge, is what the Soul is reaching for.

Our Soul is the creator and the creation simultaneously. That is the paradox. We are in continual creation as the creator. The painter that is the painting.

We have painted ourselves as the original sin, when in truth, we are part of original conception. The Soul, a continual reminder that we are the masterpiece experiencing itself. Nothing more than a molecule in the ocean of the universe, multiverse, the omniverse. Nothing less than the omniverse in perpetual imagination.

Stories In Winter

Every life is fraught with stories. Stories of an existence beyond the memories of the mind.

Some come to me in dreams, while others hang on the edge of a formless thought.

All seem lost beneath a blanket of fresh fallen snow. Wisps of a time just beyond my reach, peeking like the last blades of grass rendering for the final breath of light.

There they lie. Absorbed by an ever-changing landscape of experiences and speculation.

Most seem unattainable, but all lend qualities we can not yet ascertain to this momentary stop in this, our cosmic journey.

The passages of time will continue to fall, and all in it's path will seem forever a formless image, but beneath the qualm that shifts and reshapes like the accumulations of snow dancing in the wind, images will expose but a paltry piece to add to an ever-amassing puzzle.

It matters not, these stories painted white on white. For me they are indulgences in which to bind meaning and excitement to a life already permeated with expansion. The inspection, though full of enthrallment and promises of magic, allows for a momentary solace like one would use a puzzle. To gaze searching for the next piece of a work that will never truly be done but, will tantalize me to attempt its grandeur, non the less.

So as my eyes peruse the geometrics of winter descending weightlessly on the breeze, I configure yet another specimen to an already abundant story. Each segment coming to a momentary cessation upon which to discover and speculate what may lie within each spatial branch of an already miraculous essence.

The Welcoming

This was written for our dear friend and Tribal sister, Cathy Kidd, who dances with the angels and in our hearts everyday. Cathy's immeasurable joy is forever felt with each soulful dance and each blessed kiss of the sun.

It is a moment of clarity,
the Welcoming.
A moment breathed into space that releases all of our conformities. All of our striving's.
All of our fears. All of our misconceptions pressed upon us in this, the vast denseness of life.
The Welcoming shows us the perfection we always have been. Are.
It welcomes us back to clarity, light and home.
The lenses are released and Love embodies us once more.
What is thought as the end, is the beginning.
Freedom is what we are beyond the confines of the body.
The Welcoming.
Our home before the stars.
The Welcoming.
Our mother before the womb.
The great birth and rebirth of our very existence.
The Welcoming,
to remember that we already were, will be, and are.

The Universe at my feet

It reflects upon the snow,
The Universe at my feet

It speaks to me
beyond the language of our time.

A language that the heart understands and the mind misconstrues.

It is here in the space between space that the veil is lifted.

Patterns arise in seeming disarray.

All that portray disconnection see the unbreakable threads.

Knowing is only limited to the willingness to learn.

Misery dances in a lovingly embrace with Joy.

Bodies long since left, rejoice with those that are in creation.

It's only by self limitations that we are limited.

Only by self love that we are open.

It is here
in the space between,
that we may begin to understand
the nature of our folly.

In the End it is Love

Love is a gift.

Love is the ultimate gift.

It encompasses and envelops. It brings with it peace and joy, hope and laughter. It brings us the promise of brighter suns. Love, in it's infinite magnitude can also bring us to the depths of our darkest hallows emerging us into our own chasms of fear and despair, hearth break, and sorrow.

Love is not only what sets forth our joy, freedom, peace and wonder, it is also what lies behind self loathing, oppression, anger.

Love is the field within the field.

For Love is infinite in all directions.

It will send us to this relentless spiral, down to the nothingness.

We will grieve and despair. This of course is not the end, for even the ocean never ceases to have waves, nor do the waves hang forever on the shore. They always come home to the embrace of their creator.

Love doesn't so much 'enter' us, as it is set forth FROM us. When we open the gate, when we acknowledge what is ALWAYS present, we allow what has always been there to fly! It enables us to see a place beyond ourselves. And we grieve, and get angry, and cry for we know, we now 'see' that life, as we know it, will not be the same. The shallow wants and searches will no longer provide us the same incomplete and unsustainable brief level of masked happiness. Some of us will fight for a foot hold somewhere, anywhere. Grasping to the slick walls of memories past and habits and routines that leave us feeling even more like a leaf blowing aimless, bound to the grasp of the wind. As always, the light hidden behind the clouds, will begin to shine. We begin to understand and embrace the freedom. The True Freedom! We become light and Love is set forth anew from us. Like a parasol seed of a dandelion, seemingly at the mercy of the summer breeze, we float. We float along with tides of change, peaceful and full of promise. Settling roots only when the Earth has called for us. For Love knows when we are ready and will set forth the wind to settle us in our existing field of peace. Yes, the most important element of Love is that which exists within us. Open the door and Love will liberate us from our self-induced depths and rejoin and recognize us home.

Love never divides, it is only man that manipulates division. Only our Ego trying to formulate a hold in a world free of restrictions that tries desperately to find flaw and imperfections.

Life, conjured by Love, is all that is truly needed.

Free, unrestricted, and bountiful Love will take you to places you forgot existed.

We are God – Love

This comes up for me time and time again; We are here to experience life in a way that can not be encountered in any other place in time and space. Completely unique and complex.

Why? I don't know. Perhaps it is how many have stated before me.

For a collective understanding of something we can not yet understand or comprehend in the confines of our present being.

I FEEL that God is Love. WE are Love. Therefore; We are God in all glory and mayhem. How can mayhem and discord be Love? Be God?

Well how better to see the light but to be immersed in the dark. Everything we can feel, see and imagine, from the smallest unseen to the vast expanse of space is God – US. Even the most critically vial of beings is Love – God. We are all Light and Dark and everything in between, it is only the choices we make on which parts we prefer to nurture that determines how much of the light or dark we will inhabit. Everyone has the element of preference.

So why would a being so perfectly Love in all aspects decide to live and experience through me, You, US?

Perhaps it is for an understanding, an experience that simply can not come from ONE BEING strolling about trying to sample everything on the buffet, but that can only come from MANY of the same BEING, being fully immersed in all the dishes. Tasting, feeling, smelling, hearing and digesting ALL that each sumptuously deep platter has to offer. Isn't that what we are taught? To fully understand something or someone you need to FULLY open yourself to it. Feel it, taste it, hear it, see it, smell it, and even more importantly, smell, taste, see, hear and feel everything in between that is hidden from the obvious.

So maybe that's what God – US is doing. Maybe that is the whole point of all these songs and dances. So, WE may experience in our unique way to add to Gods'(our) collective experience.

Love is the Seed

This is a space we all want to live in. Often it feels like we will never get there. It arises, then wanes all the while we are left feeling disheartened because we were unable to keep ourselves in a space of Love.

What we have failed to see, or what we have chosen to overlook, is that no matter the state of emotion we are enthralled in, it is all derived from Love.

Love is essentially the seed in which all else grows.

Happiness, peace, non judgement, wonder....Love

Anger, jealousy, loathing, disappointment....also Love.

How possibly could the latter list be Love??

As I have come to feel, is that Love is the center of a wheel. Outward it spreads the spokes of all emotions that we are capable of.

Anger is simply Love it a somewhat skewed form. It is what arises when we fight the flow of Love. Generally, when we feel anger towards a person, place or object it is due to passion. We Love an idea so much that when it doesn't come into fruition as we anticipated we find ourselves angry. Angry for the thought, Angry for what we perceive is the reasons it didn't come to be. Angry at ourselves for allowing this to happen, not happen. Disappointed, even enraged, depending on the situation. Love in anything other than its original form is simply Love Disempowered.

It all comes down to Love.

We Love children and animals, how could this injustice be allowed to happen.

We Love Nature, why are people unwilling to see what destruction we are doing.

We Love, we Love, we Love.

All the while we will call it by another name. Lashing out in a multitude of ways. Drawing inward and festering, reactive and explosive. All because we Love.

I don't say that it is okay to be destructive but be understanding. This is where you are today. Ask yourself the questions and delve deeper. When the seed presents itself, I assure you it will be Love.

Life is Love in motion. Experiencing all in every way possible. We need only to recognize this and then flow willingly to it's understanding depths.

A Night Sky

*A black sky has come,
always present looming just beyond the reaches of sight
until ready.
Could be said that it is ominous, cold... dark... clinging to
the skin much like gum on hot pavement.
But..... There it is.
A hint...
Just enough to make my eyes question its existence.
Each moment revealing a wee bit more.
Yes, it's the light.
The light whispering of moments gone by.
History not to be found anywhere else.
Suddenly the realization dawns.
I am so small, so intimately a minuscule spec of sand on
the beach of life, but they also remind me how necessary
the specs are.
Each one a twinkle of hope,
a mesmerizing glance of light on it's way.
Each one together producing a picture of life full of
magic and light. Collectively bringing an understanding
no words will ever convey.
Proof that even in a space enmeshed in shadow,
there will forever be light.
Guiding and constant.
Sending a continual stream of love, if only we would
choose to feel it.
To know it.*

.

Follow your heart

As messages received in meditation are always important, I find myself compelled now to put them in writing, not just store them in the recesses of my mind and heart.

While journeying between our earth plane and the cosmos, I visited both. For both are integral to my, our, existence. Both are pivotal to our development and accession. Collectively they are symbiotic and essentially one.

This visit brought forth a simple message.

'Follow your Heart, not the Teachings'

Simple and straight forward.

As I mull this over, it does not say to me that teachings are inconsequential to our development, it states the opposite.

We have been gifted with teachings of all kinds during all ages for a purpose. They are consequential and essential but are tools for each being to absorb in a way that is unique to each individual.

How I process the teachings of any gift will inherently be different than the individual beside me.

It is our **Heart**, the seat of our own soul, that knows the path in which we must go. Each converging and disbursing in perfect sync. Each must set forth a path predestined for that individual.

No wrong.

No right.

No judgement.

So 'Follow **your** Heart, not the Teachings'. Let the **Teachings** be merely a sign post on your **Heart** path.

To my Children

To my beautiful children, Bailey and Lane.
You both are an endless stream of wonder,
knowledge and inspiration to me.
Without you I may not have had the courage
to speak and live my own truth.
Bailey, who reminded me that with imagination
saying, 'the sky is the limit' was
essentially imposing a limit.
Lane, who continuously shows me the value
of having your own mind. And to you both for
reminding me the importance of non-conformity
and authenticity each and everyday. Thank you.

In light of all that is going on in this world of ours, this is my pledge to you.

I promise I will Not buy you everything that you want. Not all the latest and greatest just because your friends have them.

No, I will Not buy you something every time we walk in a store just so you will not throw a fit in public.

I promise that I will Not let you do whatever you want.

I promise that I will Not allow you to disrespect your elders or peers.

I promise that I will Not pay you to clean your room, take out the garbage or any other 'chore' around our HOME.

I promise you that you may Not sign up for an activity then drop out 2 weeks in "because it's boring".

I promise you that you may Not spend your weekends glued to the TV or video games

I promise you that I will not accept 'I don't know" or "Nothing" as a good answer

And as an added bonus, No I will Not let you survive on convenience.

I Won't let you do all these because I Love You.

But I will....

I promise I Will teach you the joy of nature and imagination.

I promise I Will show you the magic of life.

I Will teach you to respect and love yourself

I Will teach you that the greatest gifts don't come from a store, and most of them you can't see, but you sure can feel.

I Will teach you the value of kindness and respect.

I Will teach you to see the wonderful uniqueness and love that resides in every living being.

I Will kiss you in front of your friends, heck I will kiss them too, so that you will all understand that love is to be shared OPENLY and without restrictions.

I Will teach you that true strength lies within.

I Will teach you that mistakes are a gift where you will obtain the most knowledge and growth.

I Will teach you that there is ALWAYS something to hope for, dream for and be thankful for.

I Will teach you that each day is a gift and full of possibilities.

I Will teach you that it is more important and effective to 'lend a hand' that it is to write a cheque.

I Will teach you to navigate with you heart and not rely so much on your mind. In fact I Will teach you how to find the balance.

And I Will do all this because I Love You.

As your Parent...

I promise that I will not grow stagnant and set in my ways.

I promise that I will not become stuck in beliefs.

I promise that I will do the best I can with what I know... In turn I also promise to always continue to learn more.

I promise that I Will make mistakes, but We will always be able to learn from them.

I promise to listen to what you are saying.... especially the things you don't say.

I promise I Will learn more from you than you may ever learn from me.

I promise that I Will be your Mother first.... but that role will constantly be changing

I promise that I Will lead by example.

I promise you that even when you are unable to see your greatness I Will

I promise that I Will probably not be conventional, or like other mom's, but you will never doubt how much I love you

I promise you that there will be a time where I may no longer hold you but know that I Will always be with you.

These are my promises to you, so that you may see that there is always Hope, Love will always triumph, and Peace is a journey of the soul not a destination, and no matter what I will always Love You.

Love,

Mom

X's and O's to the moon and back :)

Sometimes it is the awareness of singularity that becomes overwhelming. Knowing that communion lies beyond, and it is the longing for the comforting embrace of oneness that sends me spiraling. It is in this singularity that I know the richness and expansiveness. It is in this momentary movement that will yield the connection. Solidify the unsolidifiable.

The awareness of solitude brings the realization of one. Together one and the same. Solidarity then, becomes linear and perceptive.

Communication with words becomes the clothes to cover an already perfect being.

Awareness that true communication and communion is not reliant on words. The truth resides in the space beyond the original thought. Where language as we have evolved to believe, does not exist.

True communication and communion is inexpressible here on the plane of thought. It lies beyond. Loneliness then, becomes another thought in a wardrobe of thoughts.

Ruby Koevort

Want to help the Earth and humanity?

LOVE YOURSELF.

When you can truly love yourself you then are able to radiate that to the Universe, Earth, Humanity and all beings!

You no longer become 'Just one person', YOU BECOME ONE!

And this, my friends, is One Earth.s' theory of Relativity

Life.

A magical space of wonder.

A gift of endless possibilities.

Life itself, an incomplete thought.

We busy ourselves with endless tasks and self-induced responsibilities. Never fully reaching a definitive conclusion to our purpose.

The wholeness of physical presence is far too vast. No one method, or path, truly holds the infinite layers of our existence. It is always incomplete. This is validated by our ill designed, self imposed, state of 'living'.

Even after we depart, a part of us lingers. We set forth on some unknown adventure that one can only speculate.

Contained.

Uncontained.

Always as creation itself. Incomplete and ready for the next piece.

All of my work feels like there is more. Never quite the whole picture. Always yearning to be expanded upon. Perhaps that is the point. To be fully complete would defeat the purpose of a life, that in it's essence, is experiential and in continual expansion.

So, with this in mind, I have put together the following passages. Not as the beginning, nor as the end of contemplation, but as the interludes to incomplete thoughts. Always room to try and find a beginning or propose an end. No more or less than One Minds' Book of Incomplete Thoughts.

Wonderfully Incomplete in itself...

Ruby Koevort